YOUNG ATHLETE'S EDITION

THE ATHLETE'S PREPBOOK

10 Clinically Guided Exercises to Enhance Mental
Toughness, Mental Wellness, and Performance for
Young Athletes in Competitive Sports

By Natalie Graves, AM, LCSW, CADC
Clinical Expert for Athletes
Licensed Sports Social Worker

To Ivan: My number one supporter, forever crush, boyfriend, aka husband, for ALL you do, I dedicate this book to you.

CONTENTS

DIGITAL WORKSHEETS

Scan this QR code for access to digital
versions of all the forms and worksheets
in this book PLUS a bonus

Athlete's Vision Board!

https://artisanal-designer-8301.ck.page/f6bc344784

PURPOSE OF THE PREPBOOK

What Does the Word Prepbook Mean?

The word "Prepbook" in this context refers to this book specifically—one designed to help young athletes prepare mentally for their sports competitions. Before a competition, I would say we need to "prep," meaning we need to prepare mentally. *The Athlete's Prepbook* is the guide created to assist student-athletes in managing and assessing their mental well-being before, during, and after their sports seasons. The Prepbook focuses on improving performance by taking care of mental wellness.

The Athlete's Prepbook is divided into two main sections: Mental Toughness and Prepbook Worksheets. It features a range of questionnaires, mental exercises, and techniques designed to help athletes optimize their performance. By completing the worksheets, athletes can gain a deeper understanding of themselves, and implementing these exercises can help enhance their performance in competition and life. The goal is always to be mentally healthy while performing at your best.

To Competitive-minded Student-athletes:

The Athlete's Prepbook provides quick and easy techniques for setting goals, improving mental skills, establishing routines, and completing mental exercises to boost performance. Everything in this book is based on my many years of experience helping athletes perform at a higher level. Worksheets are included to aid athletes in performing at their peak during their season.

The Athlete's Prepbook also features inspirational quotes from athletes and others. The book also provides a QR code for accessing extra worksheets to use each season as well as a bonus vision board worksheet. The book aims to empower athletes to take responsibility for their own success in sports.

Let's get started!

PART ONE: MENTAL TOUGHNESS

Key Points
- **Athlete Self-Check Questionnaire**
  ◇ Self-Screener
  ◇ Athlete Inventory
- **Mental Toughness Techniques**
  1. **Goal Blitz:** Season, Performance, Practice, and Next Season Goals
  2. **Self-Talk Success:** Unlocking Your Inner Competitor
  3. **Affirmation Amplifier:** Think, Speak, Repeat
  4. **Breath of Victory:** Harness the Power of Deep Breathing
  5. **V3:** Elevate Your Performance With Visualization and Mental Imagery
  6. **Mediate and Chill:** Harmonize Your Mind, Body, and Spirit
  7. **Mindful Flex:** Find Your Zen in Your Sport
  8. **Mental Pregame:** Mental Routine Before You Compete
  9. **Reset and Rise:** Bouncing Back Stronger Than Ever
  10. **Performance Rewind:** Unlocking Your Potential Through Debriefing

  BONUS: Visual Breath: Amplify Performance Through Deep Breathing and V3

STARTING WITH THE UNDERSTANDING OF YOU: QUESTIONNAIRES AND SCREENINGS

Understanding Yourself: Questionnaire and Assessment

Embarking on a journey to enhance your performance involves understanding yourself on a deeper level. How you perceive yourself plays a significant role in how you perform. You can boost your performance by gaining insights into who you are as an individual and as an athlete. You also can begin to think about your overall wellness. This self-awareness journey begins with answering questions about yourself.

Self-Screener:

This questionnaire aims to help you assess your mood, daily functioning, self-care habits, motivation, and social interactions.

Athlete Inventory:

The Athlete Inventory provides a platform for reflecting on the past season and preparing for the upcoming one. It encourages you to identify your core values, recognize your strengths and areas for growth (avoiding the term 'weakness'), and anticipate potential challenges.

The process of self-discovery and performance enhancement is crucial for student-athletes like yourself. These tools can help you understand your emotions, daily routines, self-care practices, and motivation levels, leading to improved performance both on and off the field.

Additionally, the Athlete Inventory offers student-athletes the opportunity to reflect on past achievements, identify core values, celebrate strengths, and pinpoint areas for growth. By reframing challenges as growth opportunities, you can better prepare yourself for the challenges that lie ahead in your athletic pursuits.

Name:_____ Date:_____

SELF-SCREENER

When answering the following questions, think in terms of the weeks leading up to this season:

• On a scale of 1-10 (with 1 being the lowest and 10 being the highest), what is my mood when thinking of the upcoming season? _____

Circle one:

1. I am able to manage daily/weekly responsibilities (i.e, school, practice)

Never   Rarely   Sometimes   Often   Always

2. My self-talk is positive

Never   Rarely   Sometimes   Often   Always

3. My self-talk is negative

Never   Rarely   Sometimes   Often   Always

4. I make good decisions about my nutrition

Never   Rarely   Sometimes   Often   Always

5. I am social with friends and or teammates

Never   Rarely   Sometimes   Often   Always

6. Whenever I can, I do something fun just for me

Never   Rarely   Sometimes   Often   Always

7. I get enough sleep

Never   Rarely   Sometimes   Often   Always

8. My relationships are healthy

Never   Rarely   Sometimes   Often   Always

9. Overall, I am motivated to do what I need to do this upcoming season

Never   Rarely   Sometimes   Often   Always

If your mood is 6 or better, that is a good mindset to be in going into the season. If you answered Never, Rarely, or Disagree in some questions, ask yourself what changes are needed. If you answered Often, Always, or Agree, you are currently in a good mental space for this upcoming season.

ATHLETE INVENTORY

When answering the questions, take time to think about last season and this coming season.

1) On a scale of 1-10 (with 1 being the lowest and 10 being the highest), how committed was I to my sport last season? And how committed am I, going into this season? Is there a difference between last season and this season? Why or why not?

_____

_____

_____

_____

_____

_____

2) On a scale of 1-10, how serious did I take practice last season? How committed am I this season to practice? Is there a difference between last season and this season? Why or why not?

_____

_____

_____

_____

_____

_____

3) What are my core values as an athlete?

_____

_____

_____

_____

_____

_____

4) What are my strengths as an athlete?

_____

_____

_____

_____

_____

_____

5) What are my growth areas (we do not use the word weakness instead we use the word growth)? How can I improve in this area?

_____

_____

_____

_____

_____

6) What are the challenges I face this season? How will I address these challenges?

_____

_____

_____

_____

_____

7) Looking at last season, is there anything I want to do differently this season? Is there anything I want to continue with?

_____

_____

_____

_____

_____

_____

MENTAL TOUGHNESS

In this chapter, we will explore the ten techniques I teach athletes in my private practice with exercises to use (I have a bonus for you too). While some of these ideas might already be familiar to you, others may be entirely new. These principles have played a crucial role in helping athletes develop a deeper understanding of themselves and improve their performance. I have successfully applied these techniques to athletes of various levels, including professionals, college athletes, Olympic hopefuls, high school students, and youth athletes. These techniques have proven effective for individuals participating in both individual and team sports, regardless of gender.

When athletes work with me to improve their performance, we always start by focusing on developing a competitive mindset. A strong mental game is essential for enhancing athletic abilities. Mental toughness training is just as important as physical training; together, they lead to better performance.

For athletes, mental toughness is a state of mind in sports. It is demonstrated during pre-season, regular season, and postseason, as well as in challenging circumstances like injuries and rehabilitation. Mental toughness positively influences performance by boosting the drive to compete. It requires commitment, courage, and focus.

Practicing mental toughness helps athletes stay engaged and determined, especially in high-pressure situations. It also improves mental focus and promotes a positive, determined mindset. Mental toughness isn't limited to sports; athletes who adopt this mindset can also apply these skills to other areas of life.

Mental toughness can be developed over time with practice, similar to physical skills. It originates from an athlete's beliefs, attitudes, and thoughts. I call it BAT for short, which is an effective method for cultivating mental toughness.

B.A.T. Method

• **BELIEFS** – This refers to an athlete's self-perception as a fighter and competitor. Belief is nurtured during off-season training and in-season practice. It isn't solely based on weekly wins and losses but is built through hard work before games, matches, meets, and so on. One must commit to putting in the mental effort to be mentally strong. What are some of your beliefs? What are some of your beliefs about yourself?

• **ATTITUDE** – This encompasses an athlete's collective beliefs, emotions, and feelings toward sports-related events. Attitude directly influences behavior and performance. A mentally tough attitude can positively impact a play or change the outcome of a game. A strong attitude is developed through an athlete's internal approach to their sport, coach's attitude, values, and mission. How is your attitude going into this season?

• **THOUGHTS** – Whether positive or negative, thoughts can significantly impact an athlete and their mindset. Positive thinking is crucial for mental toughness. When focusing on your thoughts, you can train your mind to avoid negative thinking and reject negative feelings actively. Focus on things that are within your control. Practice quickly letting go of mistakes and emphasize the events that go well. Adopt a "next play" thinking pattern instead of dwelling on past actions. Are your thoughts helpful?

Developing mental toughness is a skill that should be practiced regularly. The BAT Method can be applied every day of your season and in your life outside of sports.

Here are some ways to develop mental toughness:
- Adopt the BAT Method (Beliefs, Attitude, and Thoughts)
- Identify feelings by labeling emotions and connecting with how you feel
- Learn from mistakes by focusing on the lessons they offer instead of dwelling on the negatives
- Embrace difficult situations and mentally commit to fighting through them
- Set and work towards goals, as goal setting plays a significant role in mental toughness development (more on this later in the section)

Beliefs: *What positive beliefs do you have about yourself as an athlete?*

_____

_____

_____

Attitude: *What does your positive attitude look like?*

_____

_____

_____

Thoughts: *List some of your positive thoughts.*

_____

_____

_____

Important Note About Mental Illness:

There can be a misconception that an athlete struggling with mental illness cannot be mentally tough. Mental illness is a medical condition, and anyone can develop one. It does not make an athlete mentally weak. As demonstrated by the BAT Method, an athlete can have a mental illness (such as depression or anxiety) and still possess all the attributes of mental toughness. Athletes like Michael Phelps and Naomi Osaka, who have faced mental health challenges, have achieved extraordinary success in their sports.

Now let's get into the 10 Mental Toughness techniques (plus one bonus on page 35).

"The only person who can stop you from reaching your goals is you."
–Jackie Joyner-Kersee, Olympic Gold Medalist

1. GOAL BLITZ: SEASON, PERFORMANCE, PRACTICE, AND NEXT SEASON GOALS

As an athlete, setting goals is something you're likely familiar with. When first meeting an athlete, I always ask "What are your sports goals?" This question is important because it determines our focus and actions. You need to ask yourself this same question.

Goal setting is crucial for reaching your next level of performance. It's not just about stating your goals; it's about documenting them in a place where you can refer back to them. Setting goals before competitions increases the likelihood of better performance. Goal setting creates self-accountability and focus. It's okay if your goals change; what's important is having a general idea of what you want to achieve.

Benefits of Goal Setting
There are numerous benefits associated with setting goals:
- Improved focus and confidence
- Determined mindset
- Identifying areas for improvement
- Providing a sense of purpose
- Increased likelihood of success

The Goal Blitz includes four types of goals:
1. **Season Goals:** These are the overall objectives you want to achieve by the end of the season.
2. **Practice Goals:** These goals are designed to keep you focused during practice. They can include mental cues, effort levels, and attitude.
3. **Performance Goals:** Performance goals are set before each game, meet, match, or competition. They can include specific scoring targets, desired stats, mental skills to develop, and more. These goals can remain the same, be slightly adjusted, or completely change from week to week.
4. **Next Season Goals:** These goals will be written after the current season is finished.

Let's start with your upcoming season's goals first. Think about what you want to achieve overall during the season.

Here Are Examples of a Goal Blitz:
Season Goals:
- I will improve my free-throw percentage.
- I will make the all-conference team.
- I will improve my overall attitude.
- I will improve my personal record.

Performance Goals:
- I will score 10 points.
- I will nail my landing.
- I will stay calm.
- I will play good defense.

Practice Goals:
- I will listen to my coach.
- I will be a hard worker.
- I will be positive.
- I will treat my teammates with respect.

Next Season Goals:
- I will work on getting stronger.
- I will develop my leadership qualities.
- I will improve my mental game.
- I will have a competitive mindset during difficult situations.

Complete the Goals Blitz worksheet on page 13. Scan the QR code on page 44 to get a worksheet for future seasons.

TAKE A TIMEOUT

How do you think goal setting will help your performance?

_____

_____

_____

_____

_____

Name:_____ Date:_____

GOAL BLITZ

Season Goals List:

_____
_____
_____
_____
_____
_____

Performance Goals List:

_____
_____
_____
_____
_____
_____

Practice Goals List:

_____
_____
_____
_____
_____
_____

Next Season Goals List:

_____
_____
_____
_____
_____
_____

"The only one who can tell you 'you can't win' is you and you don't have to listen."
–Jessica Ennis-Hill, Track and Field Olympic Silver Medalist

2. SELF-TALK SUCCESS: UNLOCKING YOUR INNER COMPETITOR

Self-talk, both positive and negative, can be automatic and can change based on how someone feels in the moment. Often, when I meet with athletes, a lack of confidence is a problem. Sometimes, they do well in practice but not during games. I always want to know what athletes are saying to themselves. You can block your success without even realizing it.

What you tell yourself really matters. We all have conversations with ourselves every day. It's important to think critically about what we're saying and thinking. Positive self-talk can be very beneficial for your performance, while negative self-talk could seriously hurt it. Negative self-talk stems from fear, doubt, and low self-confidence. You should always aim for positive self-talk.

Examples of Negative Self-talk:
- "I'm stupid."
- "I'm going to strike out."
- "I'm not good enough."
- "I can't do it."
- "She's better than me."

Examples of Positive Self-talk:
- "I am prepared."
- "I am ready."
- "I believe in myself."
- "I am focused."
- "I will have fun."
- "I am a hard worker."

Self-talk is tied to how you feel about yourself, and it can affect your performance. Be aware of what you're saying to yourself. A good way to judge your self-talk is to ask if you would say that to someone else. If not, you probably shouldn't say it to yourself.

The term "affirmations" is sometimes confused with self-talk, but they're not the same. In the next section, we'll discuss affirmations.

TAKE A TIMEOUT

Think and reflect: Write some examples of your current self-talk. Ask yourself if it is positive or negative. If it is positive, keep it going. If it is negative, become conscious of it and change it!

_____

_____

_____

_____

_____

_____

_____

_____

_____

_____

_____

_____

_____

_____

"Start with the mind and your game will follow."
—Natalie Graves, Sports Social Worker

3. AFFIRMATIONS AMPLIFIER: THINK, SPEAK, REPEAT!

Some people use the terms self-talk and affirmations interchangeably, but they are not the same. Affirmations are deliberate, focused statements created with the intention of highlighting ability, skill, and belief, and they are recalled at set times throughout the day. It is neither random nor based on fear or doubt, like self-talk can be at times.

I teach athletes how to use affirmations, especially when they are in season. I have done this with college teams, too. During the session, we spend some time working on personal sports affirmations. The athlete decides what works best for the situation and how it feels, and they plan when to say them. We also discuss why affirmations are important. The creation of affirmations is a positive and empowering experience. Using affirmations assists with mental toughness.

I like to encourage athletes who have never created an affirmation before to brainstorm first to see what statements resonate with them, and then, we can build from there. They can also start by thinking about what they want to achieve and creating their affirmations from that perspective. Sometimes, athletes prefer to have a set of affirmations as an athlete as well as other sets of affirmations for other parts of themselves. Both are equally important and effective.

How to Create Affirmations:
1. Brainstorm what you want to say to yourself.
2. Focus on a skill or personality trait or pull from the core values you stated in your Athlete Inventory on page 8.
3. List what you like about your abilities, talents, or skills.
4. Start forming short sentences or phrases.
5. Pay close attention to how you emotionally connect with each sentence or phrase. If it feels positive, go with it!
6. Choose three to five statements.

Here Are Examples of Affirmations:

- "I am ready."
- "I am prepared."
- "I trust my training."
- "I am mentally strong."
- "I am mentally tough."

How to Use Your Own Affirmations:

Find a place where you can view your affirmations every day. This could be a sticky note on your mirror, a note in your phone, or an audio recording you play back to yourself. Then, decide when you want to say them, at least once during the day (more is even better). I recommend it when you wake up in the morning and before you go to sleep; I call it "when the head hits the pillow." Practice repeating your affirmations every day during the season.

**Complete the Affirmations worksheet on page 18.
Scan the QR code on page 44 to get a worksheet
for future seasons.**

AFFIRMATIONS

Use this space to brainstorm:

What do you like most about your abilities, talents, or skills?

_____

_____

_____

_____

_____

_____

_____

Now, select 3-5 new affirmations:

1. _____

2. _____

3. _____

4. _____

5. _____

"One way to break up any kind of tension is good deep breathing."
–Byron Nelson, Professional Golfer

4. BREATH OF VICTORY: HARNESS THE POWER OF DEEP BREATHING

Most athletes are familiar with deep breathing, but not enough are aware of its many benefits. Sports like swimming and track and field focus on how to breathe while competing. However, deep breathing can be used to help all athletes **before** they perform. It is also a great coping mechanism for emotional management. Many of the elite athletes I work with have incorporated a deep breathing exercise into their routines.

Deep breathing calms the body down by slowing the heart rate. There are many benefits associated with this technique, particularly for athletes. Deep breathing reduces stress and pain, and it helps the body recover from soreness by making your muscles relax. Regularly practicing this technique can reduce blood pressure and increase lung function. It can also produce a more focused mindset.

You can use a deep breathing technique when you feel under pressure during a game or if you have pregame jitters. Add it to your pregame routine (a concept we will discuss later) or whenever you want to focus or relax. If used routinely, you will begin to quickly notice the many positive effects, including extended relief from worry and stress. Breathing exercises can be completed in no time, and the benefits can be felt immediately, physically and mentally.

Below are **two different** ways for you to practice deep breathing. One is meant for daily use, and the other is meant to aid specifically in sleeping and relaxing.

Exercise 1: Daily Deep Breathing

This exercise can be used in two different ways. One way is as a daily routine. It will help you start your day off right and set the tone. Use it as a way to quiet the mind and relax. It can also be used moments before you compete. I recommend making it part of your pregame routine.

Step 1: Sit up straight in a relaxed position.
Step 2: Close your eyes.
Step 3: Clear your mind of all thoughts.
Step 4: Breathe in deeply and hold for 5 seconds.
Step 5: Slowly breathe out for 3-4 seconds.

Repeat steps 1-5 at least 3-4 times.

Exercise 2: Long Exhale Breathing

I recommend using this exercise the night before you compete or when you feel worried or stressed. It will help reduce anxiety and improve sleep.

Step 1: Lie on your back with your knees bent and feet flat on the ground.
Step 2: Place one hand on your stomach and take a few relaxed breaths.
Step 3: Lengthen out the inhalation and exhalation until you have a 1:2 ratio.

Continue for 5-10 minutes.

"All that matters is how you see yourself."
-Israel Adesanya, Professional Mixed Martial Artist

5. V3: ELEVATE YOUR PERFORMANCE WITH VISUALIZATION AND MENTAL IMAGERY

Visualization and mental imagery are powerful techniques that can significantly benefit athletes. Visualization involves creating a mental picture of an event or action in your mind. Mental imagery, on the other hand, goes beyond visualization by engaging all the senses, including hearing, taste, touch, and smell.

In my practice, I recommend a technique that combines both visualization and mental imagery specifically designed for young athletes, which I call Visualization/Mental Imagery Times Three, or V3 for short.

Here's How to Utilize V3:
1. The night before a game, meet, match, or any other important event, take some time to visualize yourself performing at your best. See yourself executing the necessary skills and techniques with precision. Then, imagine the sights, sounds, smells, tastes, and sensations associated with the event (adding this step is very important). Focus on the specific mechanics and form related to your sport to help ingrain the correct techniques in your mind.
2. Repeat the visualization exercise when you wake up in the morning of the game or event. Reinforce positive images of success and mentally rehearse your performance. This will help set a positive tone for the day, enhance your focus, and boost your confidence.
3. Right before the game or event, take a few minutes to engage in visualization and mental imagery once again. This final session will help you enter the competitive environment with a clear and focused mindset. Picture yourself executing your skills flawlessly and achieving your goals.

Using V3 three times before a competition—the night before, the morning of, and right before competing—can help you improve your focus, performance, and confidence. Being mentally prepared plays a crucial role in enhancing overall performance and confidence in sports.

TAKE A TIMEOUT

Take a moment to think about how you can use V3 for your next game, meet, competition, etc.

_____
_____
_____
_____
_____
_____
_____
_____
_____
_____
_____
_____
_____
_____
_____

6. MEDIATE AND CHILL: HARMONIZE YOUR MIND, BODY, AND SPIRIT

Have you ever wanted to clear your mind or calm down before competing? Maybe you were so hyped up right before a competition and really needed to relax your mind and body.

Meditation can help you with this and more. There are a variety of benefits to using meditation for athletes. It helps with better focus, alleviates some of the strains that come with physical training, improves recovery, reduces stress, and helps you calm down.

What Is Meditation?

Meditation is a mental exercise that has been practiced for thousands of years in various cultures and traditions around the world. It is often associated with spirituality and mindfulness but does not have to be used in a religious way. Through meditation, individuals aim to achieve a state of deep relaxation and heightened awareness.

The practice typically involves finding a quiet and comfortable place to sit or lie down, closing your eyes, and focusing your attention on a specific object, word, or even just your breathing. As thoughts arise, you acknowledge them without judgment and gently bring your focus back to the chosen point of attention.

Meditation can take many forms. Each approach has its own techniques and goals, but they all share the common purpose of cultivating a calm and focused state of mind. I have done guided meditation with individual athletes and with entire teams.

Benefits of Meditation for Athletes:

Meditation is a practice that can bring many advantages to athletes. By training the mind through meditation, athletes can improve their mental and physical well-being, enhance their focus and concentration, manage stress, regulate emotions, and perform at their best.

Here Are Some Key Benefits of Meditation for Athletes:
- Improved focus and concentration
- Enhanced mental resilience
- Stress reduction
- Emotional regulation
- Increased body awareness
- Better sleep quality
- Enhanced performance

Remember, meditation requires regular practice to see significant benefits. Consistency and patience are vital to unlocking the full potential of meditation for athletes. I recommend the meditation called **Conscience Breathing Meditation.**

In this meditation technique, you simply focus on your breath. It's as simple as that. This method, shared by meditation expert Davidji, is to breathe in slowly while counting to four, hold that breath for a count of four, exhale slowly while counting to four, and then hold the out breath for a count of four. Repeat this four times, and you'll have finished a one-minute meditation, which is excellent for beginners. Gradually add more time each week as you make it a daily habit. You'll start to see results soon!

Follow These Steps:
1. Find a quiet, comfortable place to sit or lie down.
2. Close your eyes if you feel comfortable doing so.
3. Take a slow and deep breath in through your nose while silently counting to four in your head (1...2...3...4).
4. Hold your breath for a count of four (1...2...3...4).
5. Slowly exhale through your mouth while counting to four (1...2...3...4).
6. Hold your breath again for a count of four (1...2...3...4).
7. Repeat this process three more times for a total of four breath cycles.

As you breathe, try to focus only on the sensation of your breath entering and leaving your body. If your mind wanders, gently bring your attention back to your breath without judgment. After completing the four breath cycles, take a moment to notice how you feel.

Remember, it's okay if your mind wanders during this practice. Just gently guide your focus back to your breath each time. With practice, you may find it easier to concentrate and experience the benefits of meditation.

"...it's a way to listen to the self...it sets me up for the rest of the day... it's a way to observe the self."

–Kobe Bryant, 5 time NBA Champion

7. MINDFUL FLEX: FIND YOUR ZEN IN YOUR SPORT

I love teaching athletes mindfulness. I have written and spoken about mindfulness. I have practiced mindful meditation exercises with NFL, NBA, college, and high school athletes. The youngest athlete I introduced mindfulness to was an 11-year-old gymnast. Any athlete can learn to be more mindful, and being mindful will help you perform better. Mindfulness is a powerful tool that can help athletes improve their performance.

What Is Mindfulness?

Mindfulness involves being fully present in the current moment and accepting it without judgment. By practicing mindfulness, athletes can reduce stress, manage performance anxiety, improve focus, increase self-observation skills, and enhance their interactions with teammates and coaches.

Here Are Three Mindfulness Exercises to Practice:
1. Mindful of All Senses

The key to practicing mindfulness is to stay focused on the task at hand and avoid letting your thoughts wander. If you find yourself getting distracted, gently redirect your attention back to what you were doing. It may be more challenging than it seems, but with practice, you can improve your ability to concentrate. This exercise trains your mind in a unique way and helps strengthen your concentration skills.

1. Find a piece of candy with a wrapper, like a peppermint or a Jolly Rancher.
2. Close your eyes and start opening the wrapper.
3. Pay attention to the sound of the crinkling wrapper.
4. Hold the candy in your hand and notice how it feels.
5. Slowly place it in your mouth, focusing on the smell and taste.
6. Practice this exercise for two minutes then gradually increase it to five minutes.

2. Mindful Small Object Observation

This activity requires even greater focus than the previous one. In addition to staying present with an object, you need to pay attention to all the details of that object. While it's easy to get distracted, try your best to stay fully focused on the object you are observing. Pay attention to its shape, color, texture, and any other details that stand out. The goal is to keep your mind engaged with the object and avoid letting your thoughts wander. By practicing this exercise, you can enhance your ability to observe and concentrate on the task at hand.

1. Find a small object, such as a pen, paperclip, or coin.
2. Hold it or place it next to you.
3. Observe all the little details of the object.
4. Stay focused on the object for one to three minutes, ignoring any distractions.
5. The goal is to keep your mind present on the object throughout the activity.

3. Mindful Observation (Outdoors)

This observation activity takes place outdoors, ideally in a park or during a scenic walk. The goal is to pay attention to the nature that surrounds you. You can either walk or find a spot to stay still for a longer period of time. Take the time to observe and appreciate the natural environment. Notice the sights, sounds, and even smells around you. Look for details that might often go unnoticed, like a beautiful flower or a bird perched on a tree. As you observe, try to connect your mood and feelings with what you are experiencing. Remember to stay present in the moment and enjoy the beauty of nature.

1. Sit, stand, or walk outdoors, preferably in a park or during a scenic walk.
2. Notice what you see, hear, and smell in your surroundings.
3. Take time to observe the nature around you.
4. Pay attention to something that may be easily overlooked, like a flower or a bird in a tree.
5. Connect your mood and feelings with what you are observing.
6. If your mind starts to move ahead, gently bring it back to the current step and stay present.

These exercises help athletes develop their ability to focus, stay in the present moment, and cultivate a calm and focused mind. Practicing mindfulness regularly can have a positive impact on athletic performance.

"Today I will do what others won't so tomorrow I can accomplish what others can't."
-Jerry Rice, NFL Super Bowl Champion, Wide Receiver

8. MENTAL PREGAME: THE MENTAL ROUTINE BEFORE YOU COMPETE

Many years ago, I worked with a student-athlete who struggled with severe anxiety before games. To help calm their worried mind, I created the Mental Pregame Routine. Now, I use this technique regularly with athletes at all playing levels. When I ask athletes about their pregame routine, they often mention listening to music. While that is a good practice, I encourage them to go a step further.

Creating a Mental Pregame Routine provides a sense of control and confidence. Athletes appreciate having a clear plan and knowing what to expect before they compete. While you can't control everything in a sports situation, you can control how you prepare for it.

What Is a Mental Pregame Routine?

A Mental Pregame Routine is a series of tasks and behaviors that help you become calm and focused before your game, meet, competition, or other important event. Having a routine creates a mindset free from distractions and allows you to commit to your game plan and goals, which leads to better performance.

Mental Pregame Development

As part of my preparation for games, fights, tournaments, or what have you, I try to understand what an athlete is thinking. During the week of the competition, I want to know their thoughts. An athlete's thoughts (as mentioned in the self-talk section) are a good indicator of how they will perform. I ask questions like, "Where are you mentally?" and "What are your thoughts on how you want to perform?" I focus on preparation during this time. Consider your mental approach as it relates to being a competitor.

Here is a sample Mental Pregame routine:
Night before:
- Perform deep breathing exercises.
- Visualize yourself performing well.
- Repeat positive affirmations.

Morning of:
- Visualize yourself succeeding in the game.
- Repeat positive affirmations.

On the drive to compete:
- Listen to music.
- Decide if you want to talk to others or keep to yourself.

Before it's time to perform:
- Take deep breaths to calm yourself.
- Remember your goals.

Here Are Some Suggestions to Develop Your Mental Pregame Routine (choose the ones you like):
- Create a special pregame playlist.
- Review your list of positive affirmations.
- Review your game goals.
- Use deep breathing exercises.
- Use mediation exercises.

Write Your Mental Pregame Routine in the Space Below:
Remember, developing a Mental Pregame Routine can greatly enhance your performance and give you a sense of control and confidence.

Night before:_____

_____

Morning of:_____

_____

On the drive to compete: _____

_____

Before it's time to perform:_____

_____

"Champions keep playing until they get it right."
-Billy Jean King Hall of Fame Tennis Champion

9. RESET AND RISE: BOUNCING BACK STRONGER THAN EVER

The purpose of a reset is to gain perspective after a previous performance that was not successful as you had hoped and to make necessary adjustments during the season. Resetting is often needed when a season feels long or is nearing the end.

Resetting can also be used when athletes are mentally tired or feeling uncomfortable due to upcoming events like playoffs or nationals. While the specifics of resetting may vary for each athlete, it can be effective in improving performance during or after a difficult time.

Here Are Two Ways to Use Resetting to Enhance Your Performance:

1. During Competition:

Things can move quickly, and mistakes can happen. Sometimes, the current plan may not be working as expected. Taking a quick reset between points or plays is appropriate in such situations. Athletes can regain control by taking a short pause to regroup and reset. For example, a tennis player can slow down the pace of the match when their game plan isn't effective, allowing them to change tactics or observe their opponent's strategy. Similarly, in volleyball, an athlete can communicate with their teammates on the court, stating what needs to be done or encouraging readiness before the opponent serves. These quick resets help refocus and improve performance in real-time by making immediate adjustments based on what has happened so far.

2. Toward the End of a Season:

When an athlete has been playing for a long time and feels tired or stressed, resetting can help them get back on track. It's like taking a breather to think about how things have been going so far in the season. This reflection can help them figure out the best way to move forward and do even better.

Resetting is like using a unique exercise to boost performance by looking closely at what has already happened and deciding what to focus on next. It might mean going back to the basics or working on getting mentally ready. Whether it's a quick reset during a game or a big reset after a long season, it can give athletes new ways to see things, make changes if needed, and do their best when it counts.

In the space below, list the times you can use a "Reset and Rise" to improve your performance, regain focus, and get back on track:

_____
_____
_____
_____
_____
_____
_____
_____
_____
_____
_____

10. PERFORMANCE REWIND: UNLOCKING YOUR POTENTIAL THROUGH DEBRIEFING

When I work with athletes during their season, I emphasize the importance of mental preparation before and after a competition. Investing mental time and effort into the process to perform at the highest level is crucial. In addition to developing a Mental Pre-game Routine (as mentioned on page 29), Performance Debriefing can further enhance performance. This technique draws from my training as a clinical social worker, where reflecting, exploring, and processing with clients is essential.

Performance Debriefing is a process I created to examine a recent performance from both a mental and emotional perspective. It is one of the easiest yet most effective methods to improve performance. When a game, match, or competition doesn't go as planned, it's important to take some time to review what might have gone wrong and make the necessary corrections.

How to Use Performance Debriefing:

Start by exploring your thoughts and feelings. Then, examine what occurred during the performance on that day. It could be a problem with mechanics (physical) or struggles with emotional management (mental). Think about both the mental and physical aspects of your performance.

Follow these steps to help debrief your performance:

Step 1: Identify the specific area of your performance you want to focus on (preferably during your most recent performance).

Step 2: Reflect on your performance from a mechanical standpoint. Ask yourself questions related to the fundamentals of your sport and write down the answers. Here are some examples of mechanical questions from actual clients:

- How was my defense?
- How was my body positioned?
- Did I maintain proper foot alignment?
- Did I execute the correct leg movement?

- How was my follow-through?
- Did I breathe in short, quick breaths?

Step 3: After answering the mechanical/fundamental questions, take time to consider the feelings, thoughts, and emotions you experienced during the performance. Write them down and make connections between your emotions and your performance.

Step 4: Now, ask yourself internal questions related to your performance. These questions focus on your thoughts, feelings, and emotions. Here are some examples:
- Did I stick with my Mental Pregame Routine?
- How was my mental toughness?
- Did I stay focused?
- How was my emotional management?
- Were my thoughts positive or negative?
- Did nervousness affect my performance?
- Did I get distracted? If so, by what?
- Was I able to calm my mind when needed?

Step 5: After answering both the mechanical/fundamental and internal questions, reflect on the data you've gathered. What did you notice? What can you do to improve your fundamentals and emotional management? In Part 2 of this book, you can find a Performance Debriefing worksheet to assist you in this process.

By engaging in Performance Debriefing, you can gain valuable insights into your performance and make targeted improvements. It allows you to evaluate your game's physical and mental aspects, leading to enhanced performance on the field or court.

Use this space to debrief a performance:

_____

_____

_____

_____

_____

_____

_____

"I use visual breath before warming up for every outing. It helps get my body and mind in sync before going to perform."

-Collin Amsden, College Baseball Player

BONUS: VISUAL BREATH: HARNESSING THE POWER OF DEEP BREATHING AND V3

Visual Breath is a technique I developed while working with a college baseball pitcher—a talented athlete I had been working with for multiple seasons. Inspired by his dedication to improvement, I introduced him to two important skills: deep breathing and V3 (visualization and mental imagery). After a season of use, he combined these techniques to help him better perform and manage his emotions. I called the technique Visual Breath.

Combining these two techniques creates another powerful exercise for success in sports and everyday life.

Let's start by understanding the importance of deep breathing. As mentioned on page 19, deep breathing is a simple yet effective technique that can help release tension, calm the body, slow down the heart rate, reduce stress and pain, and promote muscle relaxation. It's beneficial for emotional management and overall well-being. As mentioned on page 21, visualization and mental imagery involve creating vivid mental pictures, engaging all your senses, and imagining yourself performing at your best at least three times before a competition.

How Does Visual Breath Work?

Visual Breath combines deep breathing with V3 for even greater benefits, helping you visualize your performance in a focused and relaxed state.

To fully benefit from Visual Breath, set aside 1-2 minutes each time you use it. Find a comfortable place, close your eyes, and visualize the skill you want to improve. Picture it clearly in your mind, engaging all your senses. Spend 30 seconds on this visualization. Then, add slow, deep breaths—inhaling through your nose and exhaling slowly through your mouth—while still visualizing your ideal performance. Continue this for another 30 seconds to one minute.

Here's a Complete Routine to Use Visual Breath Before Competitions:

1. **Night Before:** End your night by visualizing and mentally rehearsing your performance, incorporating deep breathing. This will help set a positive tone and enhance your focus in a relaxed state.

2. **Morning of the Competition:** Start your day by visualizing and mentally rehearsing your performance with deep breathing, reinforcing positive images.

3. **Pre-Performance:** Just before the game or event (i.e. in the car or bus on the way there) engage in another round of visualization, mental imagery, and deep breathing. Picture yourself executing your skills flawlessly and achieving your goals, entering the competition with a clear and focused mindset.

By regularly practicing Visual Breath, you can develop a powerful tool for managing stress, improving focus, and enhancing your performance. Whether you're on the field, in the classroom, or facing everyday challenges, Visual Breath can help you excel and reach your goals.

CONCLUSION

In conclusion, remember that mental toughness is not just a trait you are born with but a skill that can be developed and honed over time, similar to a physical skill. By incorporating the techniques and exercises from this book into your routine, you are taking a proactive step towards enhancing your performance, building resilience, and achieving your goals on your terms.

As you embark on this journey of self-discovery and performance optimization, remember that setbacks are not failures but opportunities to learn and grow. Stay committed to your mental wellness and well-being, and trust in the process of developing your competitive mindset.

With dedication, practice, and a positive attitude, you have the potential to unlock your true capabilities and thrive both as an individual and a student-athlete. Believe in yourself, push beyond your limits, and never underestimate the power of mental preparation in reaching new heights of success.

So, let's get started on this empowering path together! Embrace the challenges, celebrate the victories, and always strive to be the best version of yourself. The world is waiting to witness your greatness—go out there and shine bright like the competitor you are destined to be! When you are ready for the next level, the original *Athlete's Prepbook* is waiting for you to delve into.

PART TWO: WORKSHEETS

Key Points
- Performance Debrief
- Stress Log
- Gratitude Log
- Digital Worksheets
- Helpful Resources

Name:_____ Date:_____

PERFORMANCE LOG

Use this worksheet to help you reset from your last performance. When debriefing your performance, think in terms of how you were mentally and with your fundamentals/mechanics. It is important to stay positive and learn where you can improve. It is counterproductive to be negative and unforgiving of yourself. Instead, be determined to work on your growth areas (we do not use the word weakness instead we use the word growth).

1) How were you feeling the day before the performance (it is normal to be nervous)?

_____

_____

_____

_____

_____

_____

_____

_____

_____

2) Did you follow your pre-game routine? How did this affect your performance?

_____

_____

_____

_____

_____

_____

_____

_____

_____

3) Describe your performance.

_____

_____

_____

_____

_____

_____

_____

_____

_____

4) What did you do well?

_____

_____

_____

_____

_____

_____

_____

_____

5) What can you improve upon?

_____

_____

_____

_____

_____

_____

_____

_____

Name:_____ Date:_____

STRESS LOG

SPORTS RELATED STRESS

-
-
-
-

NON-SPORTS RELATED STRESS

-
-
-
-

1) List how stress presents itself in your body (i.e., headaches, body aches, trouble sleeping):

_____

_____

_____

_____

_____

_____

2) List how stress affects your mood, feelings, or emotions (i.e., anger, irritable, tired):

_____

_____

_____

_____

_____

_____

3) Indicate the following that you may need more of:
- ☐ Sleep
- ☐ Healthy eating
- ☐ Having fun
- ☐ Connecting with friends and family
- ☐ Mental and physical rest
- ☐ Other_____

4) Indicate the following that you may need less of:
- ☐ Late nights
- ☐ Fast food
- ☐ Social media
- ☐ Loud noises
- ☐ Negative interactions
- ☐ Other_____

5) List self-care activities you can do to reduce your stress:

_____

_____

_____

_____

_____

_____

GRATITUDE LOG

Research shows that giving gratitude enhances psychological health and reduces negative emotions. Giving gratitude increases feelings of happiness and reduces depression. It also aids in putting things in perspective. As an athlete, it is easy to focus on the daily grind of your sport and forget other things that matter.

This exercise is created to prompt you to think of things you are thankful for but may have forgotten. One log is for your sports life and the other log is an overall general form.

Read the following statements and write what is important to you:

General Gratitude Log:

- Appreciate when _____
  _____
- Love when_____
  _____
- Value when _____
  _____
- Thankful when_____
  _____
- Happy when_____
  _____
- Grateful when_____
  _____

Sports Gratitude Log:

- Teammate(s) I appreciate is _____
  _____
  _____
- What I like about my team is _____
  _____
  _____

- As an athlete I am grateful for _____

  _____

- As an athlete I am proud of _____

  _____

- One of my strengths is _____

  _____

- Something I have overcome _____

  _____

- Being an athlete I am thankful for _____

  _____

  _____

DIGITAL WORKSHEETS

Scan this QR code for access to digital versions of all the forms and worksheets in this book PLUS a bonus

Athlete's Vision Board!

https://artisanal-designer-8301.ck.page/f6bc344784

HELPFUL RESOURCES

Helplines
- **National Suicide Prevention Lifeline:** Dialing 988 will route callers to the National Suicide Prevention Lifeline.
- **National Alliance on Mental Illness (NAMI) Helpline:** Dialing 1-800-950- (NAMI) 6264 to talk with a Helpline Specialist when you need support, information and resources. Can also text HELPLINE to 62640.
- **Crisis Text line:** In a crisis, text HOME to 741741 to connect with a Crisis Counselor and text to WhatsApp.
- **SAMHSA's National Helpline:** 1800-662-HELP (4357) for individuals and family members facing mental health and/or substance use disorders. This service provides referrals to local treatment.
- **National Helpline for Gambling:** call or text 1-800-522-4700 for those seeking help for a gambling problem.

Mental Health Directories to Find a Therapist
- **Therapy for Black Girls:** https://therapyforblackgirls.com/ online space dedicated to encouraging the mental wellness of black women and girls.
- **Therapy for Black Men:** https://therapyforblackmen.org/ provides information and resources for black men about why and how to access mental health services.
- **Psychology Today:** https://www.psychologytoday.com/us browse and find profiles of therapists in your area.
- **Clinicians of Color Directory:** https://www.cliniciansofcolor.org directory is full of various racial and ethnic backgrounds as well as training and treatment styles.
- **Laxtinx Therapy:** https://latinnxtherapy.com national directory mission is to destigmatize mental health in the Latinx community.

Specialized Resources for Athletes
- **Courage First Athlete Helpline** is the first athlete helpline supporting athletes impacted by abuse. Call or text 1-888-279-1026. Live chat is available.

www.ingramcontent.com/pod-product-compliance
Lightning Source LLC
Chambersburg PA
CBHW071242090426
42736CB00014B/3193